SAVOR ETERNITY
ONE MOMENT
AT A TIME

Saint Julian Press

Poetry

Praise for SAVOR ETERNITY

"Alfred K. LaMotte is truly the rarest kind of alchemist. With each poem in this exquisite collection, he weaves ordinary words into pure gold, inducting the reader into a direct experience of the sublime ineffability of life itself. Sourced from the depths of his own awakened heart, his words will pierce straight through to your own tender heart, igniting and awakening you. LaMotte stands with Rilke, Rumi, and Hafiz in beckoning our souls to awaken. Let each poem be a mystery that you discover and savor as you would a lover."

~ Tina M. Benson, international bestselling author of

A Woman Unto Herself: A Different Kind of Love Story.

"The poetry of Alfred K. LaMotte speaks to my soul of long lost love, and redeems my heart from a fall that I cannot even remember. Somehow he makes the total mystery of existence feel all right."

~ Susanne Marie, meditation guide and founder of

Transformation Through Presence™.

"Inside this poetry is the deep perfume of God, a vast pool of light and pure generosity. Here are bees, honey, and simplicity of Being. That is why every time we read his poetry, we are nourished, uplifted, and we never tire of reading them again and again."

~ Guthema Roba, poet, author of *Please Come Home*

and *Wake Up and Roar*

"Alfred K. LaMotte's writing simply and actively opens the heart, inspiring and enlightening without ever a heavy-handed word of preaching or lecture. In pure authenticity and elegant vulnerability, he writes with the clear heart of a true meditation teacher, and shows us the way."

~ Diana Lang, Author of *Opening to Meditation*, Huffington

Post columnist, and director of LifeWorks Center for

Growth in Los Angeles™.

"This is a stunning and prophetic book, courageous in its commitment to the living milk of the Mother, disturbing our complacency and our stagnant idealization of who She is or how She must appear. These poems joyously report that here, and right here, is where we taste the cardinal fulfillment of our essential nature. The Feminine, as a psychic force, reaches far beyond biological sex, and thus cannot be wholly claimed by the female voice (tempting as this might be after centuries of inequality and abuse). In his new book, Alfred K. LaMotte speaks from a breadth and wholeness that is the undeniable sign of Her presence. These poems help us see that the creaturely and the divine are not eternally set apart: they can be recognized as a single gesture of invitation to a much finer, more generous participation in the real."

~ Britt Posmer, painter, performance artist and poet,

author of *The Angel and the Heretic*.

SAVOR ETERNITY

Poems

by

Alfred K. LaMotte

SAINT JULIAN PRESS
HOUSTON

Published by
SAINT JULIAN PRESS, Inc.
2053 Cortlandt, Suite 200
Houston, Texas 77008

www.saintjulianpress.com

ISBN-13: 978-0-9965231-4-1
ISBN: 0-9965231-4-6
Library of Congress Control Number: 2016937041

Cover Art Credit: Rashani Réa
Author Photo Credit: Liz LaMotte

❖

PREFACE

❖

❖

COUNTLESS STARS illuminate the night behind our eyes, whether we sleep, dream, or wake. This inner sky is purest Presence. It is wonder, both the source and goal of every mystical path.

This spacious depth in us is our connection with the Creator. And when the inner silence vibrates, we participate in the Logos, the resonance at the source of creation. As I feel it, this resonance is the essence of a poem. To immerse in the vibrant energy of a good poem is to participate in the primal act, the Word of God.

The delicious problem of the poet is to report on this inexpressible space of amazement, as it shines through the most ordinary creatures in the world; not to separate the ordinary from the transcendent, but to celebrate how ineluctably one they are, like the color blue and the emptiness of the sky.

In a time when "religion" is not trending in poetry, I dare to be a religious poet. As an interfaith chaplain, I use poetry to gather many radii into one center, honoring the mystic poets of Islam, Christianity, Hinduism, and Shamanic earth-centered traditions. There are echoes of all these paths here, Christ and Mary Magdalene in the Easter garden, Shiva dancing with Goddess Shakti, the wine of the Sufi's ecstatic annihilation, the Pagan's path of return to the Mother through a hollow gourd...

To discover the transcendent in the sensuous, and the voluptuous in the transcendent, is a task that pervades the mystical poetry of both East and West. To probe this mystery, poets of all wisdom traditions have used the nuptial language of Lover and Beloved. I do not shy away from speaking traditional religious language in these poems; nor do I shy away from finding Buddha-nature in a moldering dog turd.

"Be still and know that I am God," wrote the Psalmist. These poems celebrate the oscillation of our inner stillness in waves of "I" and "Thou." Yet the play of Lover and Beloved is ultimately the play of Subject and Object in every act of perception, beat or beatific. The suchness of your gaze in mine, or a fallen festered apple in the autumn sun, is the locus of amazement, where mere seeing transcends duality. The poet simply reports on this phenomenon.

If my poems evoke even a momentary dissolution into wonder, it is all I wish for you, friend. That moment is eternal.

Finally, please know that these poems encompass loss as well as fullness. I honor your dark night of the soul, reader, because darkness is not the absence of light, but the womb of light. Whether we name it "kenosis," using the New Testament term, or "sunyata," the Buddhist word, self-emptiness is finally the loss of who we are not, not who we are.

The spirituality of abounding joy, and the spirituality of self-emptiness, are never two separate ways. Let loss be the illuminated door.

Alfred K. LaMotte

TO MY TEACHERS
MAHARISHI MAHESH YOGI
AND SRI SRI RAVI SHANKAR

CONTENTS

"WHEN I AM SILENT I FALL INTO THAT PLACE
WHERE EVERYTHING IS MUSIC."
~RUMI

"TO BE SPIRITUAL IS TO BE AMAZED."
~RABBI ABRAHAM JOSHUA HESCHEL

SAVOR ETERNITY
ONE MOMENT
AT A TIME

GENTLE

A gentler world begins
in the way you touch your heart.
Be soft with the light inside you.
Caress your body with this breath.
God is nothing else
but the place where the sun comes up
in your chest.
You are the glimmering destination.
You are the golden honey daubed
on the bread of the ordinary.
Whatever is perfect,
whatever is heavenly,
begins here.

LANDSCAPE

This nakedness my native ground,
a wild forgotten garden gone to seed,
your wheaten undulations rilled
to breasts of brown by slow dark-silted time.

Ancient disciplines of listening thrilled
your vales with lark song; deft seeing in-laid
each pale iris with beryl and jade
chiaroscuro, a blossom for each weed.

As minstrel, I would amber you in sound.
Were I a poet I would turn you on
a rhythmic lathe to rosewood rhyme.
An artist, I would layer your dark skies

outrageously in amaranth and fuchsia,
brush the chalcedony of your thighs.
A virtuoso, I would lean
your body's chocolate swollen cello,

balanced on one foot, against mine
to hear your hollows resonate, and strum
your tautest golden string like *this*,
then gently pluck some lower, darker tone...

But I'm a lover, glutted by minutia,
glorying in dust, wandering your fallow
landscape of half-opened lips and loam,
gleaning the raindrop of your kiss.

SHED

I shed every petal,
crushed every pollen drop
to fragrance without form,
peeled the seed away
and cracked each casing
of the emerald germ
down to the black
Upanishadic hollow.
Still I could not feel you...
I relinquished every veil
of innocence and shame,
became more naked
than the moon before the sun,
offered my flesh to
the fire of wanting,
melted every photon
to its wave of night.
Still, I could not touch the love
of whom fools stammer...
So I hid in your hiddenness,
tore off my wings and
spiraled down into the rhythm
of your stillness,
fell into the sea where
breath goes before it returns.
I knelt on the shore
of my own ancient heart,
faithful to the last lost pulse.
In a wickless flame,
in a soft scarlet chaos
without root or stem,
I became infinite.
Longing blossomed
in the golden void.
I became you.

MONARCH WINGS

You send the frailest creatures
to teach me lessons of bewilderment.

Don't ask me whether a whorl
of butterflies is one or many.

I am too busy learning that gesture,
the cyclone of my heart
in the hush of a chrysanthemum,

lapis lazuli skies
in a bowl of blueberries,

cloudlessness completely sphered
in a robin's egg.

When my body can no longer dance,
my breath will leap with news
of your light.

When my breath no longer leaps,
the beaten creature in my ribs
will open and close

like these thin golden wings
veined with night,
pulsing on a milkweed.

I yearn to be nothing more.
You yearn to hear me whisper this.

Everything depends
precisely on how whirling
kisses stillness.

THREE A.M.

3 A.M.
It is important to say that
nothing matters
but the one who is always
already here, the gesture
of a magnanimous hand
sweeping the void.

Being goes on without me.
Surrender to what never sleeps.
Stillness enfolds me with
indescribable tenderness
before I am breathed.
Why not return here
with every exhalation?

No need to be reminded
when no mind is.
Love is who I am
when I make no effort
to be anything else.

Now inhalation arises,
but who is breathing?
Rest in me as I rest
in you, beloved.
We were never not pouring
into one another
like currents of stillness.

All creatures come to drink
the silence from this well
before creation.

How melodiously the planet sings
in my withering body,
the sun's brief tincture in my blood,
perpetual midnight in the iris
of the listening eye…

We are made of ceaseless vanishings,
as fragrance in a crinkled rose
or lyric in an echo, the finish of brandy
on the tongue of the Bodhisattva…

Let my bone of silence be
entwined with mushrooms and moonlight.

It is important to say
that nothing matters
but abysmal love.

Savor eternity
one moment at a time.

AGE

Dear one, you cannot reverse
this aging process.
But you can turn your breath
into light,
pouring it through
the vacant places in your body,
filling every atom like
a chalice to the brim
with the invisible sap
of eternity.
Then the Master
may drink from you.
Dear one, you are never
one moment old!

ENVIRONMENTAL BUDDHISM 101

Such a perfect afternoon for traveling
nowhere down a forest path!
Let your feet perform a miracle.
To the famished gravity of the planet,
offer healing steps.
Give a walk, don't take one.

Recycle your body, compost your mind
into worm-food, just by looking deeply.
Find unfathomable Dharma practice
in not wasting your bagel.

Marvel at void tulips under a Stop sign,
satori in a milkweed, trellised through spokes
of the Enso in a rusty bicycle wheel.

See immortal Tara's tantric face of compassion
in a month-old dog turd, tufted
with feathers of mold in the dandelions.

Lanky condom looped over blossoming heather,
Nalgene bottle impeccably thrown
into suchness among wild anemones,
garden snail's aluminum Diet Pepsi home:
Garbage reveals your Buddha nature.
Picking it up is the Bodhisattva's vow.

But if you must throw things away, remember:
throughout countless Buddha fields, vacant lots
of raindrop-pearled abandoned cars, galaxies
of Skittles wrappers roiled like cherry blossoms
in the silent heart of Amithaba,
there is no such place
as "Away."

OPEN

Blossoms don't open themselves.
It takes a sunbeam to ignite the rose.

I was asleep until you placed
a ruby on my chest

awakening the expiration
of this gentle song, the whisper

of Spring in a Winter garden.
So'ham, So'ham, So'ham...

One breath pours wine into
the burnished cup of another.

Some say that this is just
a sound without meaning.

I say it means the Magdalene
has met Jesus

in the bridal chamber
of the heart.

I WOKE

I woke this morning to discover
that a wolf had quietly stolen
in through my breath
and curled up in my rib cage.

There were elk tracks in the snow
on my belly and thighs.
I could still smell the fragrance
of bob cat, taste the feathers
of pheasant in my mouth.

Evidently a fawn had been born
in the grotto under my chin.
Its mother was foraging
through my basal ganglia.
Its wide blue pupils contained
two whole Winter skies.

No stars remained, I drank them all.
But the moon was throbbing
like an egg in the empty nest
woven of mistletoe between my eyebrows.

A siege of herons overflew the frozen
wetland of my face
clamoring at themselves reflected
in my icy stubble.

I woke this morning to remember
my chastisement and exile,
and my purest possibility:
that I have no other home,
no other body but the murk
of soil and birds, and the oily river,
and the fallow mystery of this planet.

MESSAGE FROM YOUR ANCESTORS

The ancestors want you to know
that you are not required to carry their pain.

Your mother did not spin the web that nets you;
you wove it from your own desire.

Last night's rain won't nourish this flower;
why thirst for ancient tears?

Your grandmothers are singing for you
to birth your own unbearable happiness.

Your grandfathers' bones are praying for you
to hunt the sweetness in your marrow.

Don't think you must stand like a warrior
in the withering crossfire of your father's blood.

What wounds you is your own mind's wavering
blade, slashing this moment into past and future.

If you insist on making reparations,
plant a wild pine, a tree of Presence.

You cannot pay them for the privilege of breathing,
or for awakening this solitude of beauty.

They need no libation, nor thirst for the offering cup.
They are not hungry ghosts, but merely

earthworms who luxuriate in loam,
shards of sunlight lodged in dogwood blossoms.

Do not carry them; they will not carry you.
They bear their own grief and laughter.

The past is vanishing smoke, the flame is now.
Be christened with this breath: name yourself.

You sleep in the secret chamber of your ribs, alone.
No one else enters and leaves your lungs.

A mother kissed you, a father held you;
you owe them nothing for this.

They did it for themselves; now let them
be about the business of their next childhood.

Father your heart, Mother your body.
Hold and kiss your own new sparkling babies.

Give them your grandmother's name if you like,
but not as a weight, not as a brand on the thigh,

But as a prayer, a promise of astonishment
for what has not yet been conceived.

GOSPEL

Nothing is wrong.
You have never not been free.
This is the good news.
Every photon of your flesh
is the boundless sky.
This is the good news.
You lost yourself
in the shadow of beauty
so that beauty might
find you again.
There is no bad news.
Healing comes
from a heartbroken place
where you've breathed out
everything you carried.
Stay there.
The next breath
is God's love.

AUTUMN'S DOOR

Look! Scarlet mushrooms
nippled in rotted dahlias,
crinkled leaves in moon silence,

harpsichords of dew
chiming their destiny of ice,
tiny omens of oblivion,
weightier than summer.

Thus do the angels of frolic
scatter their keys before you!
Open your nostrils now, your throat

to the sacred odor of spoil.
Don't be afraid to root in the putrid
rind and peel, spent tea and wizened
roses, webbed in veils of ghostly mold.

Find wisdom, go to the ruined garden,
where no waste is and beauty makes
use of the useless.

Ponder the calligraphy of worms.
Enter whatever is empty.
In the sepulcher of an ulcerous gourd,
smell your way beyond the shroud.

Gaze into a spider's web, that fretwork
of desolation, window to your own abyss.
Become thistledown, threaded in a breath

of November sky, careless where you root.
Follow one commandment: Be ye perfect,
ever arriving exactly where you are, precisely
at the moment you get there.

SWANS

Your heart is a lake
on which there seem to be
two swans, nearer
than inspiration and sigh...

but there is really only one
white-feathered splendor
settling gently
into its own reflection...

No need to shatter
the mirror of your world.
Just polish one another
with forgiveness...

CONVERSATION WITH GOD

Everybody seems to have conversations
with God these days, so I had one too.

"God," I asked, "I only have one question.
Why did you create all this?"

"I don't remember," God said. "Does it matter?"

"But Lord," I replied, "Philosophers search
for meaning: is there no Reason in your work?"

"None at all," said the Creator. "I'm just in love.
What more do lovers need?"

I demanded an explanation:
"Scriptures declare that you spoke the Word.
Creation was born from chaos at your command.
Doesn't your Word mean anything?"

God thought about this a moment, then replied,
"No. I was just humming."

Outraged and incredulous, I cried
"All this, all this is just a song?"

And God said, "Yes, just a melody for
my Beloved, who was quietly dancing.
She inspires everything I do.
She has been my delight from the beginning.
When the world was made, I stroked her dark hair
as she lay her head against my shoulder.
I'm not even sure of her name.
Sophia? Hakhama? Ishq'Il Haqq?
I only know, She is my Silence
whirling..."

OLD BODY

This old body has its aches and pains,
but even weeds have blossoms, sweet
peas among wild billowing poppies.

All in all, it's worthwhile having bones,
giving light a trellis to embrangle itself,
ligaments to give the stars a cranny

where they fall, root down, and lodge
their smaller selves; it's not so bad, this
swollen loam of blood and umber marrow.

We're like peaches with edible fuzz.
I can caress your belly, run my finger
down the fur, smell hay just after rain,

and watch the valley's willowy arms
enticing mist with creek whispers
into her shaded bed. All in all, the flesh

is no burden; it's good to have a body.
There is nothing illusory about it.
Even an old one, especially an old one.

This breath of dust makes prayer possible.
Not a petition for weightless space,
but thanksgiving for the place where I am.

FRAGMENTS

"Imperfection is beauty." ~Marilyn Monroe

And you have only just now
accepted the grace!
These fragments of your life,

the broken lines,
the missing phrases,
endings that don't quite

rhyme, beginnings
that die in non sequitur,
stillborn ellipses

of awkward syntax
silently holding hands
as you disappear

around corners together
alone again, until
suddenly it falls

into place
as a single poem
needing no interpretation

because the mystery
of your beauty fills
the empty spaces...

ANARKISSED

Mira, Francis, Baal Shem Tov
were anarkissed for love.
King David danced naked before the Ark.
With only a broken jug, a brick for a pillow,
Rabia refused the princes' hand:
she was anarkissed for love.

Whitman, cummings, Teilhard de Chardin,
ambulance drivers and poets
who bound up warriors' wounds,
were anarkissed for love.

Christ too, Shatterer of Temples,
who burst the old wine skin of Law
with the new wine of I Am:
so anarkissed for love!

Ferment your marrow, distill your blood,
drink who you are and burst what contains you:
the wine skins of Marx or Reagan,
the wine skins of Moses or Mohammad,
the wine skins of nations and borders.

Don't bottle your sparkling heart!
Be hard stuff, explode the rose,
uncask your loins, make the timid spin
while their governors snore in a stupor.

Why scrawl ancient constellations on
the walls of your scull like a cave man,

those starry beasts, the bear, the bull,
the scorpion and crab? Be their wildness
in your body now, anarkissed for love!

Find the meadow of intoxication
where Jesus twirls with anemones,
singing in the feral language of fragrances.

Find the garden where the lion-headed
serpent sings to the violin zebra,
winged elk fly through the ripeness
of the pomegranate, and the Bridegroom
marries the Bride with a kiss
that signifies the mingling of all juices.

This kingdom needs no king.
These laws are inscribed in the palm
of every hand that holds a hoe or soup pot.

Give up anger.
Let ideology dissolve into a tear.
The revolution is to breathe.
The radical act is to be present.
Nourish the earth with your secret joy.
Be anarkissed for love.

SMALL AS GOD

"Ano-raniyan, mahato-mahiyan: Smaller than
the smallest, greater than the greatest." ~Upanishads

God is smaller than a gnat.
God is smaller than a fleck
of pollen on a bee's foot,
smaller than a wave of gravity
in the ocean of a quark.
God is smaller than the time
it takes light to pass
through the width of a hair.
Any creature as small as God
must be un-created.
To get that small,
you'd have to contain the universe.
You'd have to disappear
into everything
and be as humble
as a last breath.
No body is as small as God.

OUT OF MUD

With obscenely gleaming fingers
they squished you out of tears and mud.
How much of that piquant glitter

did they spew into your mire?
Must you carry the stain of a God in your seed?

Muck back to mineral where the lotus grows
from dreamless mycelium sleep.
Go down with the dung beetle under a stone

and dig up the Word of creation.
Call it Light.

Find out where slugs come from.
Move inward like the shadow of a flame,
a gravedigger's moonlit shovel.

Why not make your path the dance
of calamity, your way a bursting tulip,

a windy cataclysm of thistles?
Fall backward. Trust the transparent.
Discover a lover in what is not there.

One day your progeny from a distant star
will find your gizzard preserved

among these yellow mushrooms of desire,
and pluck from your moldering soul
bright amber fragments of their ancient bones.

YOUR TASK

Does the sunbeam get tangled
in the lace beauty of the dragonfly's wing?

When spider weaves her web across the night,
does she ever snare a star?

Suffuse the world like water in a herring net,
without getting caught in the stories.

Be more and more like the ripe moon
hanging from an apple branch.

Your work is simply not to fall asleep,
the task of love.

A current of kindness will flow up your spine
to light the Milky Way,

its emerald wisdom rooted down
in the vineyard of your loins.

Drink of the shadow, taste of the fire.
Cherish the womb of a deeper silence.

Don't strive to get enlightened.
Let your grieving be the manger.

Give birth to your anointed heart,
and remember that the sun and moon

draw power and beauty from the stillness
that moves your breath.

I KNOW MY DOG IS DREAMING

I know my dog is dreaming when his legs grind like broken gears
and he barks like an embryo.

I know my cat is dreaming when she purrs with half open eyes
in which I see cities on fire, ancient towers collapsing into the sea.

I do not know when I am dreaming. Perhaps I am the butterfly
Chung T'zu mistook for himself

in a reverie brought on by eating mysterious noodles cooked
in the hut of an old woman, whose body was a chrysalis

from which the New Moon emerged like a hungry moth
to wake him up.

I once thought I was a Taoist. I once thought I was a Christian.

Now I know that my religion is what comes from honeysuckle
and alfalfa, the gold

I drip on stone-cut buckwheat groats. My religion is
the syncretism of raspberries, walnuts, and cream.

My religion is the way children and their grandparents
behave around food,

when their parents escape to the kitchen to argue in secret
desperation about the cost of staying alive.

My religion is your arms around me, mine around you,
and the willingness to remain like this and do nothing

while our hearts murmur to each other about how
hard and simple it is to ask for love.

PUMP

There should be a name
for this plump organ
swilling blood and oxygen,
spilling it all over my body,
to each little hungry globe,
this old drunken pump,
churning my animal dark
to bright, yet somehow,
in its cave of bone and
gristle of night, containing
galaxies, enfolding the swirl
of rimless possibility,
the space of the starless
Beyond not even God
has yet explored...
I call it my "heart."
But really, it's a door
to another thirst, a thirst
that has no name.

HOW NEAR

Sometimes the tumbler
is so empty!
Yet even this absence
is my love.
How near am I?
I have disappeared
into the boundless night
behind your eyes.
No need to say, "have faith,"
but simply, "be the shadow."
From the center of our tears
light is born.

DARK CHOICE

"If you wish to be sure of the road you tread on, you must
close your eyes and walk in the dark." ~St. John of the Cross

Choose your darkness.
There is a night that circles inward
like a falcon toward the place
where you despair of touch.

But there is another night,
an absence nearer than blood,
that flings you into orbit
around stillness,

where no embrace is needed
because you have become
the ever-widening solace we all seek
in the hour before dawn.

Make your breast a sheath for what
is sharper than God, what penetrates
the moist and soft. Clinging
to tenderness can be a great weight.

Be a razor with edges defined
by what is not, by what is honed away
through seven silences,
your ruthless gorgeous incisions.

The gashed forsaken animal in
your groin is not who you are…
You are the scimitar of the Destroyer,
who draws you out of his ribs, dripping

the bliss of blood burgundy, desiring
to use your violet lethal incandescence
in the formless combat of love…
To him let your viscera proclaim,

"I never knew how rich my darkness was
until it burst into flame with your Presence."
In the jar of your wound
he makes wine…

Shadows feed this fire.
Voidness is oil in your lamp.
Destitute, you lack nothing.
Evening cannot contain you.

Why not be the black circumference
to whom you prayed for light
and rest, dear love, in the arms
of a catastrophe?

EDGE OF THE POEM

The poem is a vertigo of edges,
a falling climber's secret ecstasy,
this world slipping from his grip at last.

Poetry is an extreme sport.
If you understand this spun
blue silence, you've turned

gravity into wine.
Once you leap into a poem,
rising and falling are the same.

Rabi'a, Whitman, Hafiz, Rilke
stood upon love's ledge and leapt
into winglessness,

crippled eagles in the void.
Or did they plummet like flung stones
into Basho's pond?

The sound is all that matters.
Fall with the words and crush
their meaning on your tongue.

There's no name for descending light
that curves back toward its blackest center.
This is why we sing about it.

Neither ground nor grammar count,
but the gesture of this breath, naked
with her lover, the next inhalation.

FUZZ

Your frontal cortex is overrated.
If something smells like
your grandmother's pudding,
just eat it.
If it hugs you, hug back.
If it glows green and gold
in valley mist, go that way,
following your delight.
Listen to the crinkle of your insect fuzz.
That's what caterpillars do,
and they turn out splendidly,
with wings.
Inch by inch, your belly
will invent the path,
with hundreds of meditating toes,
love's quivering antenna
tuned to the sun
by a mindless stream of photons.
The glistening stick of the Way
has many branches,
but never a wrong turn.
Bug, your goal is everywhere.

GOD OF OPPOSITES

Suppose the opposite is also true:
God is powerless.
God is seen in darkness.

God knows nothing.
God makes us hungry.
God does not say a Word.

If you fall, God gets down with you.
God flees from the mind of the theologian
and dwells in the belly of the fool.

God is unwashed, with dirty hands.
God has no idea where this is going.
God listens to your laughter as much as your prayer.

God is not interested in your good works.
God has spilling breasts and enormous hips,
giving birth without male seed.

God passionately acts out.
God does not respect sobriety.
God wanders away from churches and mosques

to find solace among prostitutes, hobos and anarchists.
God can't remember any story.
God desires your body, just as it is.

God left heaven centuries ago to dwell inside you.
God asks not for obedience but a song.
God appears on the outskirts of your empire,

in one of the old brown-skinned circle-dancing tribes.
God comforts the poor and troubles the powerful.
You crucify her.

THE HOLY INCOMPLETE

"Is anything ever finished?" ~*Michelangelo*

Symmetry shattered,
the crumpled universe
tumbles out of the vacuum.
Praise ooze in the cocoon.

Praise the worm of chaos in a pear,
the random fall of feathery thistle,
the bursting nipple of mistletoe.
praise sweet wounds
in the wizened persimmon.

Revere the accidental scattering of
light in your least favorite chromosome.
Praise the process incomplete,
the arc of beauty skewed
from its ghostly asymptote.

Become miraculous medicine,
a potion for healing distilled
from in-gathered stars and
fecund fetid forest rot.

Praise crone and placenta.
Praise your body cobbled
from perishing moments
of insignificance and surrender.

Let what you were bow down
to who you are.
Nothing is finished:
therefor Spring.

IN THE LIVING GODDESS

In the living Goddess there is no "should,"
no rule or commandment to disobey,
no one to follow down a path.

Her only recipe: make ghee
and pour it through your body.
Liquefy all things solid.

Can the earth leave its orbit around the sun?
So I cannot take my gaze from her face.
This is the bondage of love's freedom.

Remaining formless indigo, her sky
is a garland of roses and thorns.
Transparent sap takes on the tint of blood
because the mirror of her kindness
reflects our sorrow.
Silence has been wounded,
emptiness the texture of a baby's cheek

in You, in You.

Of course I could endure the Spring
without looking at a single flower,
then brag, "I am liberated from Beauty."

But I would rather drown
in the maelstrom of your eyes
because their fragrance chose me
for drowning.

Kali, make faces at me.
Stop my breath and frighten me
into enlightenment.

Serpentine Shakti with midnight moves,
seduce me into meditation.
Parvati, Goddess, don't dance with me,
dance through me, a backbone of moonlight.

We are dead bees in
each others' goblet of raindrops,
slaves of unchained sweetness.

I gladly wear the shackles of my Beloved,
virescent as a scarob's wings,
for She wears my body like a dark veil
around each inhalation.
If you do not understand this,
your lungs are bellows without fire.

Come, use the faintest feather brush
of breath on flesh to dissolve
this mind of wanting.
Drop your burden, make mischief.

Discipleship is for ants and donkeys,
but we are dolphins diving through waves
of annihilation.

Sell your flesh, blood and sky.
Barter your armor, your jewels.
Get inestimable nakedness.
You belong to someone else now.
Everything's been sold
to the Goddess of astonishment.

FOOD

"It isn't what a man puts into his mouth that makes him impure,
but what comes out of it. Saying this, Jesus pronounced all foods pure."
~Mark 7:19

I am what I eat.
I am sunlight crushed and yellow
in the Yarrow root.
I am the sinew and marrow
of a wild elk.
I am the leaping flame of a salmon.
I am air, the green kale's breath.
I am rain globed in the grape.
I am reverence for the seed.
I am fermented nectar
and the sacred hunt.
I am Chacruna leaf, Psychotria Viridis,
chewed by the shaman.
All food is God.
It is the way we grow it,
the way we follow the deer
and pray to the soul in her blood,
the way we honor life,
the way we honor death,
that makes it pure.

DANCERS

Some dancers never touch the ground,
though their feet are made of dust and rain.

I have a secret love who waits for me,
fresh from the tomb in the garden of my loins.

She's a serpent coiled around my vagus nerve,
the tree whose fruit produces wine, without seeds.

What I need with her is pure back-breaking joy
beyond the laws of matrimony.

Weary of angels, that hierarchy of whispers,
I just want a night of wing-free reckless singing,

some wild untethered kiss from the Goddess.
I've fallen off the ladder of enlightened souls,

back down to my belly button... Now don't
be shocked, I speak in a language of shadows

about things beyond the blood, more naked
than these drooping organs uplifted by myths.

Wounds, tears, the fall, exile and return
are all a drama for burnt-out lovers

who've forgotten how to dance in midnight flames.
We who are present do not require old stories.

This wild affair begins when our feet leave the earth.
We're waves of wonder now, given to wind.

Others fall back, ashes at dawn, but you and I
burn completely in a darker bluer fire.

DOWNWARD

Use the night to wash
the sunlight from your wings.

Ascending into glory
has made you stiff.

Let gravity be your prayer.
Plummet with valor.

A mother draws you down
to her umber breasts.

Mingle in the pull of that deeper love.
Cease to struggle

against what makes you heavy
and you will be weightless.

Anoint your forehead
with grass and soil.

Unpolish yourself.
Into your bright wounds rub

the tincture of darkness.
God wants to be all of you.

WANDERER'S SONG

"Be a wanderer." ~Jesus, Gnostic Gospel of Thomas

Ardent seekers follow a single path.
I wander off-trail.
It's hard to arrive when you're already here.
Vanishing without a trace is my journey.

Tell me when you get there, friend,
is anything more lovely than this falling
dogwood blossom on a silent stream
that weaves through mossy boulders
where liquid mirrors mirror the liquid soul,
whispering, "You are the way"?

Keep searching till you're
good and lost like Jesus.
Then take off your shoes and call it home.
With every barefoot step the earth says,
"Welcome!" You never even get close
to where you were going!

The only consolation is to throw away
your map, then start dancing where you are,
arms toward sunset, wordlessly praying,
never trying to name the stars that arrive
one by one, like honored guests.

Take your stand right here, but softly,
knees surrendered to the moon's weight,
bending with the heaviness of pearls
reflected in water.

Dust is your sacrament now.
Taste immortality between your toes.
Linger, but do not stay.
Be a wanderer.

YOGA TEACHER

"A baby is a yoga teacher." ~*Sri Sri Ravi Shankar*

A baby is your yoga teacher,
a flower your yoga teacher,
ice on an April pond,
dance of moth wing
un-singed by flame,
constant flow of the moon
returning to blackness,
all sharing a secret mudra,
a perfect asana, achieving beauty
through impermanence. Selah.

Your yoga teacher is a white tailed deer
who grazes on the lawn at first light
eating all your blossoms so quietly.

Your yoga teacher is a vanishing trout
in a pool of sunlight between rocks
on a snowmelt stream.

The electricity of a cat doing nothing,
or the current in a wire a bird loves
to perch on that would kill you.

Anger is your yoga teacher if you
gently stay with it in your belly,
watching the alchemy of bullet lead
dissolve into sorrow, the mercury
of tears into peace.

A sip of fresh water is your yoga teacher,
a causeless smile, gratitude for dust.

Give everything to your yoga teacher,
whose studio is the little closet
between heartbeats, where you learn
the posture of formlessness.
One breath is the price you pay
to enter this ashram.
It costs more than you could ever keep.

Your teacher is the trembling hand
of grandfather, exiled to the inaccessible
kingdom of glacial sleep,
far North of any words you whisper.
Your teacher is death, because the dead
do not drift away: they are the soil, greenly
bending up to meet the kiss of your feet.

Now listen to the most distant sound
you can hear, a mourning dove at evening
over the still lake – your teacher.

Or watch the leisurely magnificent pulse
of a butterfly wing on a cobalt sprig
of Summer phlox, suddenly startled
into disappearing – your teacher.

Take a vow to be healed
by the very next creature you meet,
your teacher, who will introduce you
to an old old friend, your Self –

this groundless falling through your chest
into the radiant abyss at the center
of all the swirling stars.

SHAMAN SISTER

On this journey through the forest
of your body, pause by a starlit pool
to harvest your milky seeds.

Find the cavern between your breasts
where the tribe of the first people greet you,
and your grandmother holds a steaming pot
of root medicine. Stay here.

It is a place of ceremony where you
will be shaman to your shadow,
priestess to the deer, herb gatherer,
keeper of Goddess-given moon rhythms.

You will heal your green womb with
chthonic tinctures of mere breathing,
bee honey guided, wave cloud hands,
make sun-moon mudras to grow maize,
improvise the dance of the uterus
over flames of blood to expiate
the sorrows of your unborn children.

Rattle throat gourd, beat djembe soul
with thighbones of desire,
pluck two-stringed kora, heart lyre
using the sun for a finger,
blow lung-deep didgeridoo and
occupy your tears…

There is no other power, shaman sister,
but the way you melt into me,
and together we get poured
as offerings into a fire
that heals the earth.

HUMAN INDEED

A poem composed on the Winter Solstice

I am human indeed.
Tonight I dwell in deep poverty.
Who knows if I will inherit
the gold that is on fire
in the ore of my chest?

Human indeed, sustained
by perpetual loss.
Tonight who knows if I
will taste wealth overflowing
from a single breath?

Indeed human, I blossom
precariously on broken stems,
thirsting for sweetness,
rooted in the dark.
Who knows if I will ever drink
the healing sap
from my own hollow seed?

I suckle an abysmal sorrow.
Who will share the breast milk
of my emptiness?

This wound does not close.
It is the eye of wisdom,
a human gash indeed.

Who knows if, tonight,
I may finally embrace
the fierce beauty of my own
beaten heart?

WANDERING TIME

Words have served their purpose.
Now it's time for brandied starlight
in plum petals, birds fermented
in vaults of holly, the burgundy between
Earth and Venus, the darker
stronger stuff of vintage silence.

It's wandering time, walk softly
in cedar amazement.
Savor the duration of a raindrop,
the ever-expanding moment
of a tongue-crushed huckleberry.

Lost all night in green inebriation,
listen as the planets sigh in pine branches.
Taste their distillate sparkle
in your heart's hollow.

Learn the art of not revealing
what you long to share
with every thirsty stranger.
Then your luster will be like the moon
pulling on gardens from within.

Love is a secret, the Beloved is a secret,
you must be a secret too,
a hidden flowering others only
scent in the darkness we all share.

Let each breath be an excess,
a sin of yearning for the blush concealed
in the modesty of blackness.
Come back tipsy, lover – do not speak
of what or whom you have known.

WHO TOLD YOU?

White and black cannot be found
in the ruins and valleys of a human face.
You're the dust in a wrinkled rainbow,
whorled pallet of earth tones,
ginger, sorrel, burnt sienna.

Who called you "white,"
that disdain for shadows,
color of the fear of falling
through the prism of contradiction?

You are not white, you are oak,
apple wood and dandelion.
Make wine of yourself.
Make a barrel of your bones.
Acquire the flavor of your ancestors.

Who called you "black,"
that abstraction of a laughing tear?
You are not black, you have sown
sunset in your cheek furrows.
You are banyan and mahogany,
kola nut and olive, cocoa bean of grief,
kinnikinnik of the sacred pipe.
You are the night.

Voracious love has dipped us both
in honey, meshed our dreams
in darkest cilia, netted our souls
like mushrooms in sweet loam,
the wild manure of one dragon.

Through innumerable pungent roots
the same juice bears us upward
into starlight.

LEAVEN

Presence is the leaven that makes earth rise.
We knead this loaf by walking gently,
honoring ecstatic raspberries
that tumble through the crippled zero
of a junked tire,

peaches fallen into putrefying splendor,
lightning of naked twigs on Autumn sky,
hieroglyphs that signify how jaggedness
resolves into awakened space.

This isn't just pretend, it's how
Christ beholds the lilies...
Let that eye of kindness lead you
back to the vulva where your clan emerged,

womb-amber chaos all our dreams
entangle in, the quintessential element
of seeing, where we suck
the nipple of original otherness.

After love making, some mother
must have swept our ashes up
in the wake of her heartbeat

where we could smell the mulch
of opposites, the musk of the dead
in a bundle of thrown-out hyacinths.

We tasted rubies and moonlight,
the bitter yeast on golden grapes
un-gleaned at vineyard's edge,
first fruits for homeless strangers,
those lovers of losing their way...

From the heat of composted loss
the packed blackness of our sorrow
suddenly sprouts bejeweled graces.

I'm still stumbling home from that
first fragrance, friend.
You're not as drunk as I am yet,
but you'll get there, you'll get there.

GIFT OF TEARS

Polish your stillness with tears.
Wander to their moonlit source.
Dip beyond enchantment.

Give thanks for what makes you
strong and soft in your nakedness,
each translucent diadem distilled

from a thousand years of pain
into one drop of presence,
finishing your eye with a light

that does not blind the soul
by judgment, but seals
all that is seen with understanding.

Observe the finest details
of the dark,
then return to the silence

where every morning
the thirsty animal of your heart
comes down to drink.

HOSPICE

Take a breath from the infinite.
Even one is immeasurable.

Now pour it back into eternity...
This is how you die.

This is how you play
with giving and receiving.

And if they call it your deathbed,
please don't worry.

It is like the deathbed
of a golden dahlia.

You too must go down
into the bulb.

PORTAL

A flower is a portal
that welcomes me home.
All Spring and Summer she leads me
through breathless sexual doorways
of trillium, poppy, hibiscus...
I do not know her name.

In Autumn I follow a grub
into the hollow squash,
a caterpillar to its mausoleum
of hope, the melancholy crow
where echoes go, enticed
by her musky dissolution.

In Winter a naked twig points
joyfully to the void.
My seeing untethered from its socket,
I enter her sky.

Two motions transport me
to one awakening: mud rising into roses,
petals crumbling to loam;
the dance, a ruthless perishing;
the adventure, delighting in dust.

I let a leaf be a leaf,
let a pebble of amber glitter in a brook
and leave it alone,
let every creature fall into its occasion,
tumbled and polished by birth and death.

This takes courage -
not to know the name of the mystery,
yet to call her the Mother.

BODIES

Inside this body made of cougar,
made of rabbit, owl and cobra,

made of minnow and dog, locust and newt,
is another body made of breath,

and of the feelings that your mother had
when you kicked the universe from inside.

In that body is a body yet more joyful,
made of light, the crystal memories of

dancing with the angels of the rainbow.
Now in this body is another, so near

you cannot touch it, yet it touches you,
a body that is never born!

Husks are filled with nectar,
zygotes with dreams, ruined castles

with the ocean that contains them.
So the perfect body of Silence contains you,

a spool of light tangled in the vacuum.
Tell me, luminous dancer, tell me, cougar,

tell me, embryonic breath, kicking
your dear mother from inside,
which body are you?

REVELATION

The old Rabbi said, "Torah contains all revelation."
The Brahmin said, "Vedas reveal everything."
"The Gospel is the end of it," said the priest.

Then I went to a Mosque where the Imam told me,
"Those old books were corrected by the Prophet:
no revelation after holy Qu'ran."

But a funny thing happened listening to those priests:
my heart contracted in a breathless withering.
I felt the juicy marrow dry up in my bones.

So I walked barefoot through my own back yard
and consulted the first plum bud,
whose tiny green nipple gushed Torah,

Veda, Gospel, Qu'ran, inebriating nectars
blushing up the twigs in my body, Allah
struck dumb by the fragrance of pollen.

The breasts of El Shaddai could not contain
the milk that spurted from blossoming limbs
and bubbled up mushrooms of curdled moonlight.

Forsythia dripped golden wine; I tippled
the tulip cup and spilled bright God
over bluebells and carillons of moss.

Isn't every dizzy atom in the wilderness
singing its song, and every mistake a libation?
Stumble to your offering, friend.

The original prophet was surely a Robin.
Then came the grace of the messenger Bee,
at night, Upanishad intoned by frogs,

ten thousand little pundits in the wetland!
At dawn I'm moved to silence
by the Sura of the Sparrow...

I cannot fathom the verses of the Thrush,
feathered rishi in the apple tree, so I peruse
the runes in cloudy entrails of evening.

Scriptures are for Winter, hieroglyphs of frost,
but when Spring comes, epistles are pronounced
in the petals of the hyacinth, the I Ching cast

in apple blossoms against the sky.
As long as seasons unfold wings of Now
from old cocoons, revelation will not cease!

ANOTHER CUP

Whatever the opposite of bowing is,
that's what you've been doing too much of.
Let the part of you that never gets married
wed eight billion lovers with a vow of amazement.

All through the black hours, be wooed
by an incoming tide, then consummate
your silence with sunrise.

Annihilate hope, be a mist
making covenant with sunbeams, disappear
without a trace in the inconceivable vastness
of the next moment.

It's not that you attain the goal, but that all
the light in the universe, falling toward you
forever, finally arrives in your body.

Enter the tavern of oblivion,
stay sober, observe dreamless sleep
with a glittering eye, single, fierce,
lit by the wine of gratitude.

After one sip, you won't remember why
you were angry; after the next,
which side you're on won't matter.

And wherever you thought you'd get
by refraining from what makes
lovers crazy, you'll get there quicker
with another cup of this!

NADEEMATI

Nadeemati: Arabic, feminine, "my wine drinking partner"

There is no confusion.
I seek promiscuous kisses

from all lips pressed to mine
in a singular quietness.

I adore as many sweethearts
as there are human faces,

beneath the veil of each,
one Mystery -

love's longing for love.
This how God calls

tremors of Herself
back to stillness.

This is the mystery of me
and why each touch is pure.

And this is why, Nadeemati,
gazing into your eyes,

I am solved.

7 INSPIRATIONS

After days of rain the sky melts into pools of cobalt, rivers of gold.

I follow the commandment of the robin: "Take seven inspirations of light; then see how you feel."

Standing nowhere special, everywhere sacred, bare feet on wet grass, I lean back and drink long body-breaths of gold.

In through my forehead, down the perineum, out through the soles of my feet: I am the sun's hollow path.

Because this fire inspires my skin, sprouts tremble with nectar. Every cell in my loam is an ocean. I am the fifth element.

Infinitesimal benevolent bacteria wriggle in the belly of the earth, moving me to meditation. They glisten, therefor I Am.

Beneath deathless stones, larvae uncurl, awakening my prayer, as my prayer awakens them. Transcendence is causation.

Once, forsythia were yellow waves of yearning in the zeal of a seed, sewn in the furrow between my thoughts.

The chasm of a peony proves that God is nothing less than ultra-violet pollen, charged with the fragrance of human desire.

My heart has two chambers, chalices of wanting, flowers of blood, full and empty.

My body is a wordless prayer; yet if words be needed, there are these: "I am the garden, You are the Spring."

I worship Shakti, the primeval dancer, in the form of soil, my own flesh, and the good worm.

YOU WILL NOT SURVIVE

When I hug you,
you will not survive.

Then my arms will release you
as from a cocoon

and two rainbows will fly out,
one brushing the heavens,

the other touching the earth,
all that remain

of your laughter and tears.
People will whisper,

"Love destroys everything
but these wings!"

MARRIED

We've all been married to each other countless times:
it's complicated.

Our prenuptial agreements gave everything
away to the ex: that's why we're poor.

It's why you feel this flame in your chest
when you gaze at the baby in the grocery store.

He was the king betrothed to your eternal soul.
The wizened crone, inching forward on her walker

like a wrinkled larva with red spots,
was the girl you ran away with, the vixen

who yearned to be a pirate's wife.
It's why that dark perfect stranger makes

the twigs inside you bud with so much nectar,
you just want to get down and do it

right here on the floor at Costco.
We're an Autumn garden of softening gourds,

crisping petals in a sunbeam, mushrooms
tangled around each others golden roots,

because in Heaven, none of us ever really
got divorced.

We're all still rolling around on a king-sized
mattress, exchanging crimson cups of wine

in our twin-chambered honeymoon suite.
What more can I say, beautiful one?

This passion preceded breathing.
You gazed at me, I was created.

We were in love before the Word
could whisper, "let there be light,"

before any God so loved the world
that he betrothed his only son.

When darkness opened its wound
to become a heart,

we taught the Creator how to sing.
We touched before there were hands.

KENOSIS

The pathless way
welcomes everything.
Even gods break open and spill.
It's how Jesus became a man.
Listen to the music
of what is not there.
It's how Miles Davis
turned silence to platinum.
Throw the seeds of all
you ever wanted away
in the fertility of stillness.
To the fiery thirst of the moon
give your blackest hour
so that night may be whole.
The void is Pinot Noir.
If you cannot taste enchanted musk
from fallen stars in the forest,
cupped in runnels underground,
you need to ferment
your darkness.

PREY

For every lethal gash in your body
there is medicine deeper inside.
Do not be afraid to bleed.
That is the path.
Let hurting make you whole again.
Become food, a balm for the wrathful.
What runs through the tunnel
in your bones is the ointment
of unending night.
Apply it, and your flesh
will illuminate the world.
Intelligence is solitude.
Keep faith in the Alone.
If you are grieving, go to the woods.
Follow your feline familiar.
Be a tawny ball of surrender
curved around your wound.
Consult the fur, your pupils
melted opals on snow.
A flame of healing will arise
from not resisting sorrow.
Nestle in yourself.
Counting your breaths won't help.
Learn to purr.
Prayer is a single expiration
of unwavering loss…
Can you hear them approaching,
the steps of the hunter
on frozen pine needles?
It is not you who hunger, but he.
Warmth flows without effort.
This is the law.
Now share your perfect blood
with a stranger.

ALL LIGHT

All light is one.
But not all light is the same.
What glows from the darker
wisdom of your tears
is your own peculiar rainbow,
its fountain deeper inside you
than the moon or Pleiades,
kindling the earth at your core,
giving the scent of a heavenly
secret when you smile...

Hold that beauty as an offering
on your tongue, but leave it
unspoken, the nameless
Eros of transparency.
Let it be the sheen on your
mahogany body.
Let it glisten also from things seen –
the sea-wide eye of a newborn seal
on a wild beach,
the paper lantern face
of your mother just dead...

Let that weightless incandescence
lift your hand in the most
ordinary gesture,
the way you stir honey into tea,
the way you wash a dish
from your father's homeland,
the way your bare feet phosphoresce
at 5 A.M. on clover, savory with rain,
the way you genuflect to a firefly,
and when the firefly is gone,
to night itself.

HONEY DANCE

Time heals all wounds, they say.
I say we are the wounds
in the green body of time.
We harden into berries,
swell, blush, fall, burst,
surrender our seed.

Grubs discover us,
restore us to death,
scrivening black letters
of emptiness into our bones,
the name of the abyss.

But we need these holes
to fill with music until
our absence becomes one
final breath, the sky.

This is the honey dance
of crystal and sap that happens
among fallen apples,
bleeding out their gold
in fissures of slow-cooked wine,
revealing the way of the worm
in the red delicious.

Through all our vanishings
a sweet amrita flows
and one bee only escapes,
laden with vestiges of late
September, the stolen treasures
of impermanence...

RAVENMOTHER

Ravenwaddles
down the shore.
Fat Yoruba Ju Ju Mama,
rattle in each claw,
rumbling haunches hunched high,
breast low, croaks and coaxes
life back over a beached whale....
Don't make fun of her cakewalk:
It's compassion.

Ravenhears
men moan from conchs and mollusks.
Lobster gods, blushing
with frustration, click their claws.
Ravenhears the croak
of sea turtles, their backbones
gashed by propellers,
seeping human plasma,
shells inscribed with faces
of our unborn children.

Ravenfeels
the wail of hungry spiders
yearning to catch moons
in their exquisite webs of emptiness.
Ravenknows the healing medicine
in poison berries.

Ravenreads cedar runes,
the scrawl of ruddy trunks
against relentless green,
transcribes coyote ululations
from a hemlock breeze.
She's Sybil to whispers of owl's wing.

Ravensleeps,
Madonna-dark, awake inside,
motherhood of motherhood,
layered in feathered crystals
of uterine night.
She is the color of silence
flickering on the whitecaps
of the void.

Ravenmother
is pregnant with unbearable
stillness...

Ravenweeps
for the world to come,
then gets down to work
pecking, shattering the clams,
freeing the voices.

LIKE A MOUNTAIN

Repose like a mountain,
flow like a river,
walk like a cloud.

Better to be the path than follow.
Each exhalation a steady flame
that burns away the past,
your chest a cloudless morning.

Spread a mantle of patience
over your bones
like a tent in the desert
where the dead may slack their thirst.

There is only one way
to the Master:
Be what the Master is.

ON MY PORCH

On my porch tonight
hummingbirds stop by to chat,
then leave for happy hour
at someone else's cherry-red feeder.

I host quieter, more constant friends,
bashful tree frogs, ascended
from the drought-ravaged pond
to summer in my flower pots.

They ask nothing but three
square inches of wet dirt
under some gardenia leaves.
I love them best of all creatures.

Did I tell you that?
Honored guests, wide-eyed
as ugly Taoist monks
come back to earth again!

I cannot say if they are thirsty
or contented, each one
smiles with such vacant
longsuffering joy...

TROUGHS

The silence of five moths on a yarrow stalk,
a prime number of dandelions,
two mallards on a pond,
a single cloud,
the sense of One alone
floating on her ocean of zeros.

The open palm of your lover's eye
offering the desert between words.

The naked observation of a lilac
untainted by its "lilac" name
in the blues of your garden.

Rain-laden Summer breeze, a wing
of desirelessness gliding
up your spine, ringing
the bell of night in each vertebra.

Vacuums, troughs of time
in the ordinary of the seasons,
where you are permitted to surrender
your argument, and breath out
everything you were against...

You could flower now and die here,
learn from the moth and morning glory
how to occupy your body
so completely.
You could create abundance
from the empty bowl
in your heart.

REFUGE

Take refuge in this moment.
One lightning bolt of silence
through the heart of a child
incinerates ten thousand books.

All the speeches of politicians
burn to tasteless ash
on the diamond tongue of a lover.
A wild hyacinth springs
from the manure pile.

All morning irises nod
in agreement with the wind.
There is no war in this meadow.
Gods yearn to be born here
for one cool April morning.

If you begin with amazement
a nameless Grace
will accomplish your day.

The daffodil knows this,
unraveling stillness.
A silent cloud can feel it,
vanishing in violet space.
The bee keels over and drops
into the amaryllis...

Why then do you have
so much trouble
merely dissolving
into what you are?

GATES

Though the gates were closed
I entered the garden
while the watchman was asleep.

I whispered the name that awakens lovers
but makes all other eyes heavy.
It's a secret syllable and we won't
say anything more about that...

All I will tell is, I arrived
where the sower is the seed,
the minstrel is so hollow he becomes

his instrument, and every sigh
is filled with a melody of fire.
Death has visited this place, but gently,
treating the soul as a sunbeam treats dew.

Surely you recall those ancient veils
that might have been a rainbow,
or fingers closing your final gaze...

Surely you remember the desolate
wedding bed, whose sheets retained
the Beloved's musk, where the dancer
became her dance...

Didn't you feel the stillness while
all else went on spinning without you?
These shadow feet left no memories.

How would you know I had been here
had I not left this poem
written in the breathless summer air
with the wings of a dragonfly?

MISTAKE

In your lattice of misdeeds
you look more shattered
and beautiful.

A treillage of cracks
on the mirror of God
makes each reflection seem
intricately winged.

One appears many there
because we dare to stumble.
Blunder gallantly, friend.

Surely, love grows vines
on the arbor of your broken places,
making nectar of sorrow.

The grape does not return to say,
"I have become wine!"
There is no turning back
from the pressing.

Ravage your heart.
Falling heals you.

MINUS

I got drunk on the gin
of subtraction.
From every creature
I deducted your Name.

From your Name
I subtracted my breath.
The remainder was mead.

Now I'm minus
the one who tasted it.
I think I might have cancelled
quiddity itself...

There is only a fragrance
of lilies, a jungle
the color of blood,

erotic green of parrot's shout,
silver glistening of toads,
evocative of death not
by violence but beauty.

I subtracted the veil
between worlds
and all that remains
is the entanglement

of my surprise....
Pay attention.
The Beloved is whispering,
"Loss teaches you everything."

MELT

You don't have to melt
until you are ready.
Remember this:

Each moil of your unoiled joints,
every numb stiff gristle of resistance,
cramp of anger, clabber of shame,

clot of envy, opinion or belief,
is simply a mass of refusal
contracted into "me,"

a particle afraid to waltz
with its field, a wave
that will not settle to its sea,

a sky who thinks it is a cloud,
a self who won't give up
I-dentity...

Don't let go until you're
ready, friend. You have forever.
Yet remember this:

To melt is not to pass away,
but to pulverize diamonds
with your dancing,

watch the spiraling fire
of your body, and witness
the whirled.

NIGHT OF THE DANCING GOD

The most sacred Yogic festival in India is Shivaratri, wedding of Shiva and the Goddess, when devotees keep vigil in ecstatic chant and meditation.

This night, prove that there is more than One.
Whet both edges of love's dagger with your breath,
then plunge it into your body.
Ask Theresa whether this pain is sweetness.
Ask the Bridegroom if longing is stronger than death.

A deft hand of diamond emptiness will sever
your crown to let the silver comet tails escape
in sighs that cannot find their alphabet.
Remain awake in jasmine-scented darkness,
your lungs a forest of broken buds whose sap
evaporates into the moon.

Shambo is a medical thorn
who removes the deeper thorn of wanting
lodged beneath your breastbone.
Where sacred rivers comingle, a maelstrom of black
gravity pours out stars; who can explain it?
She who is not afraid to become the night.

Let your flesh be the gateway of meditation,
Shiva's kiss a flare of pollen, pistil striking
stamen in the madness of the mud-born rose,
twining up the pearl espalier of your spine
out of Shakti's moon-drenched vulva.

Mingle your tears in a winepress of held breath.
To the form of the grape, the sweetest vintage
is extinction. Therefor, be crushed between
the syllables of *So'ham*, I am He! Why pretend
that you are not both Bride and Groom?

Forests, lizards, crickets, clouds, the screech
of peacocks, all ferment in your vacuum,
the glittering cask of your vigilance.

At least for now, at the nuptials
of the coiled cobra with its sacred venom,
be the diaphane where pilgrim dancers
circumambulate each other's eyes
in gyres of stillness.

Birthlessly clear, a bountiful absence
where no particle rounds its zero with sod,
be the sonorous gong un-struck, whose echo
is the sun: resonate your desolation.

Let the milk of the abyss
wash the marble lingam of "I."
Kiss the razor of your own beauty.
Let the last note of your song be a tremor
of emptiness, the shuddering breast
of Kundalini at dawn.

Then sing, *Shivo'ham!* I am Shiva;
I am bright annihilation; I am the imperceptible
nectar in whatever shines!
Just for tonight, let us dance inside each other,
veiled in silence…

Those who think they know may call it prayer.
But you and I, who suffer speechless wheeling
through onyx midnight in the marrow
of our backbone, surely name this mystery
the Wedding of the Void.

SEVERED

As many times as there are stars
I asked "Why?"
The night was silent.

Then just once I said,
"Your love."
The night became a song.

A stillness blossomed
deep in my body,
another and more secret sky.

Your touch was a blade
so whetted and
deadly soft

my heart barely knew
it had been severed
into I and Thou.

SONNET TO ROUND THINGS

"God hugs you; you are encircled by the arms of the mystery."
~Hildegard of Bingen

God hug you whole and round you with a thirst,
then crush your clustered loveliness to wine.
Having no body's arm, may God use mine
to brim your cup, my sphere of love immersed
in yours, as turquoise in a thrush's egg,
or music spilling from a vacant reed,
the circle of my breath a prayer to beg
of stars the fire to sing, of you the need.
Violets dewed with dawn's dissolving pearl
remind us to be grateful for the mere
vanishing moment, when twin souls twirl
eternally, like pollen in a tear.
Love suffers perfect loss, yet owns no less.
The more our hearts surrender, more possess.

OPUS

I hear it now, a poem of one Word,
a wild insouciant light-bearing Word
that thrills the heart of a gnat
and spins ten million suns
from the black hole of silence
on the tip of my tongue,
a Word that oscillates each atom,
quickening the hippocampus with hope
in the angry politician's reptilian brain,
a Word so hot it shocks
that veiled lady Night into revealing
the starry algorithms of her dance,
at dawn her lavender fingers
stroking the mist away... Oh
one sweet ever-echoing gong
of impeccable magic,
charged with the super-conductive
quantum uncertainty of poetic justice,
so quietly and elegantly transforming
the four horizons into one drop of honey,
even the wildest weed, the tiniest petal,
scribbled with a syllable of prayer...
Someone has spoken it: "Yes!"
Praise the murmurer.

DRINK

Dogen saw the moon in a dewdrop.
Ananda saw Buddha in a flower.
I saw Christ gazing back at me
from the bottom of the empty cup.
Some pour it all out to get here.
I got here by drinking
everything.

CREDO

My prayer wheel is the turning year,
the sun my confessor, my priestess the moon.

My daily offices are morning mist, evening swallows,
hush of midnight.

My scripture, white clouds on blue emptiness;
pictograms of geese, pointing South.

I gave up theology to watch the bees make honey.
My anointing is the mud between my toes.

The barefoot poet, Jesus, taught me to mulch and till
the heavens into loam.

His Spirit is a quietness in my heart.
Hope gets in the way; the source is gratitude.

Through vaulted arches of hemlock and cedar,
a thrush bell calls me to prayer.

May the pilgrim melt into her path, the path
into the goal,

the goal into this moment, and the very first step
into Waylessness…

POEMS ARE MAPS

Poems are maps for getting
lost in your heart
where everyone can find you.

Come and be wildered.
You don't need to ask the way.

Which way does the magnolia bud unfold?
To the East or West? Right or Left?
Please touch the whole world now.

Awaken in every direction at once.
Be the radiance you seek.

ABOUT THE AUTHOR

Alfred K. LaMotte is the author of *Wounded Bud: Poems for Meditation* (Saint Julian Press, 2013) and co-author of *Shimmering Birthless, A Confluence of Verse and Image* with Rashani Réa (Rashani Réa, 2015).

Fred has published in *The Friends Journal, Empty Mirror, Tiferet Journal,* and the anthology, *The Yes Book* (Exult Road Press 2014). His first book is being translated into Arabic. An interfaith chaplain, meditation teacher, and instructor in World Religions, Fred lives near Seattle WA with his wife Anna. He has two daughters and a golden poodle, Willy.

With degrees from Yale University and Princeton Theological Seminary, he studied contemplative prayer at monasteries in Europe and the U.S. Fred has spent decades exploring Yogic meditation as well, having personally studied with two rishis of the Vedic tradition, to whom he dedicates this book.

A Quaker, Fred has been a community service director and chaplain in Quaker and Episcopal schools; and for the last decade an interfaith chaplain at The Evergreen State College in Olympia WA. He also teaches World Religions and Philosophy for the global Distance Learning Program of Central Texas College, specializing in courses for the U.S. military. His students are deployed around the world, many in combat zones. Fred has developed an on-line teaching style that includes meditation and creative writing to deal with the life and death issues of soldiers.

Fred gathers poetry circles for seekers from different spiritual traditions, meeting at the still point, the center of the crossroads. He is dedicated to reviving the universal language of mystical poetry as a force for peace-making.

Visit his Amazon author page at: *amazon.com/author/alfredlamotte* and meet him at his blog site: *http://yourradiance.blogspot.com/*

ACKNOWLEDGEMENTS

I wish to thank my wife Anna, whose patience, wisdom and valor allow me to be who I am.

I wish to thank the journal *Tiferet: Literature, Art and the Creative Spirit* for sharing my poem, 'Revelation.' I thank the journal, *Empty Mirror: Books, the Arts and the Beat Generation* for sharing my poem, 'Message From Your Ancestors.' And I am grateful to editor Jill Cooper for including my poem 'Opus' in *The Yes Book, A Collection of Writings About Yes,* from Exult Road Press.

I am so deeply grateful to Dana Chamseddine, dearest soul sister, Lebanese meditation teacher and mystic poet, for translating my book, *Wounded Bud,* into Arabic.

Finally, in deepest gratitude, I hold up to you the art of Rashani Réa, who not only designed the cover of this book, but published breath-taking, breath-giving illustrations to my poems.

Please enjoy her meditative collages and my words in the companion volume to this book, *Shimmering Birthless, A Confluence of Verse and Image* (Rashani Réa, 2015). It is an elegant coffee-table art book, superbly crafted in deep textured color, just one of many stunning art books that Rashani offers. Visit her website: *rashani.com.*

Lightning Source UK Ltd.
Milton Keynes UK
UKOW03f1206100417

298771UK00001B/347/P